My
Prayer Journal

If found, please return to:

Name:

Contact:

This journal belongs to:

Church Details:

This Week I'm Praying For

Prayer

*I will give thanks to the Lord because of his righteousness;
I will sing the praises of the name of
the Lord Most High.*

Psalm 7:17

This week I am Thankful For

Things I Learned

My Prayer Calendar

Sun

Mon

Tues

Wed

Thurs

Fri

Sat

Notes

Prayers for our children

My Prayer

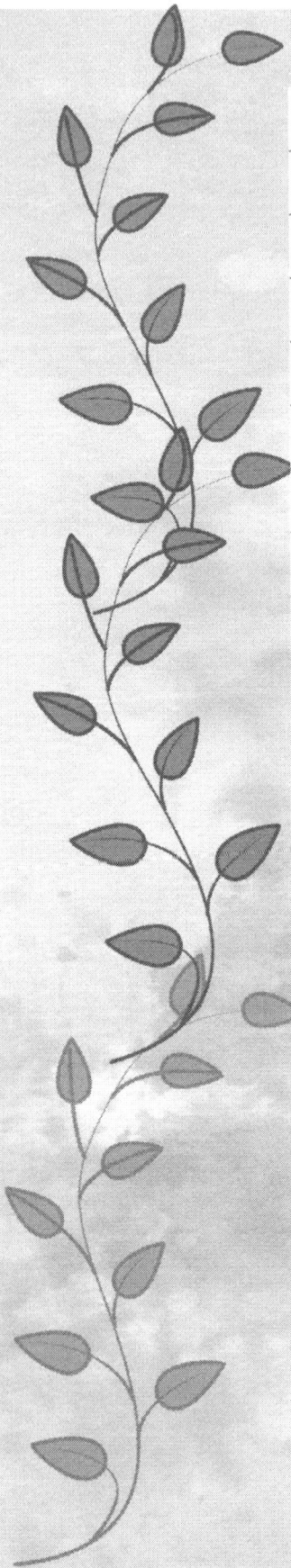

Bible Discussions

Prayer

Challenge

Person/People

Notes

Bible Reading Plan

☐   Text

☐   Text

☐   Text

☐   Text

☐   Text

☐   Text

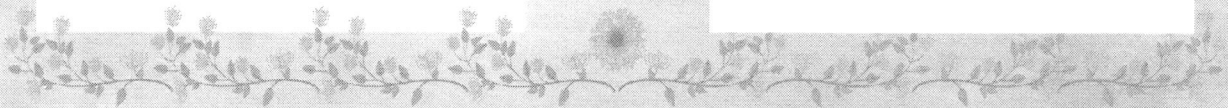

Inspirations

This Week I'm Praying For

Prayer

Come, let us sing for joy to the Lord;

let us shout aloud to the Rock of our salvation.

Let us come before him with thanksgiving

and extol him with music and song.

For the Lord is the great God,

the great King above all gods.

Psalm 95:1-3

This week I am Thankful For

Things I Learned

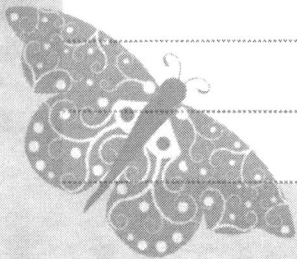

My Prayer Calendar

Sun

Mon

Tues

Wed

Thurs

Fri

Sat

Notes

Prayers for our children

My Prayer

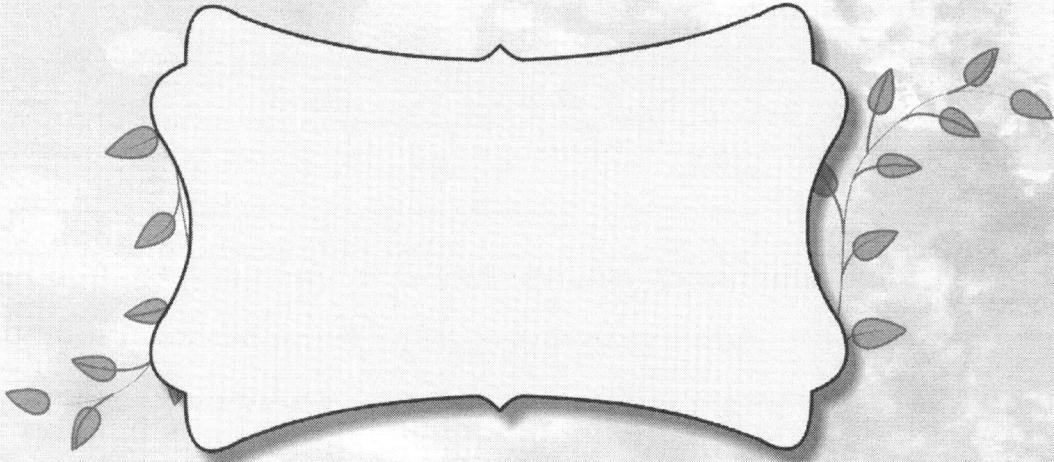

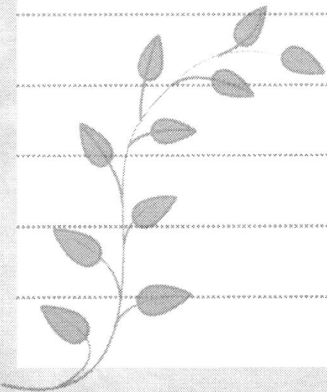

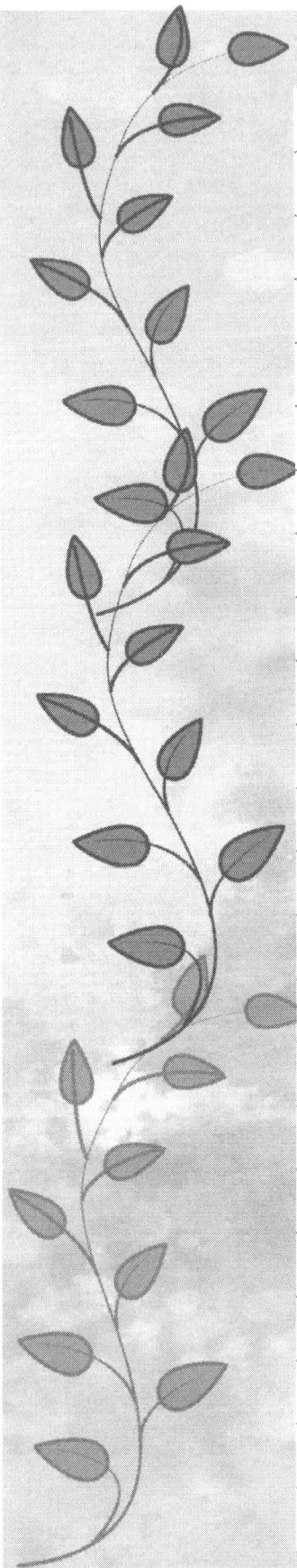

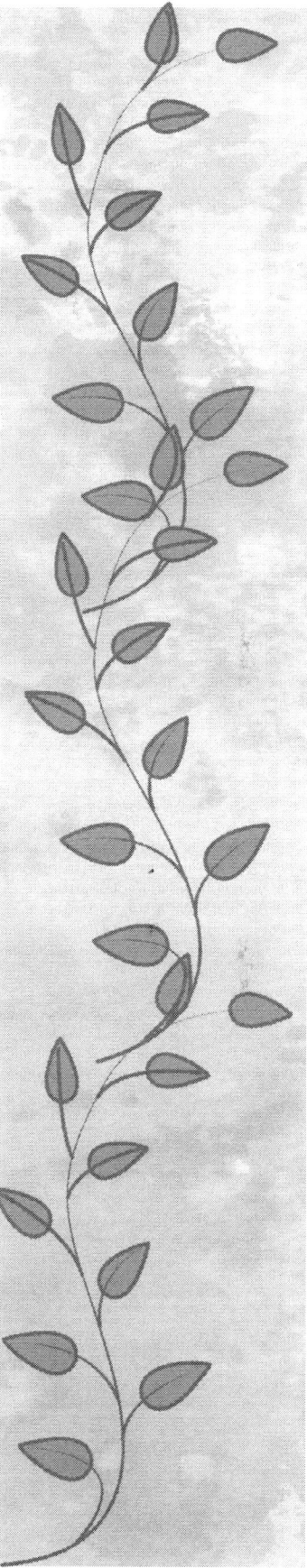

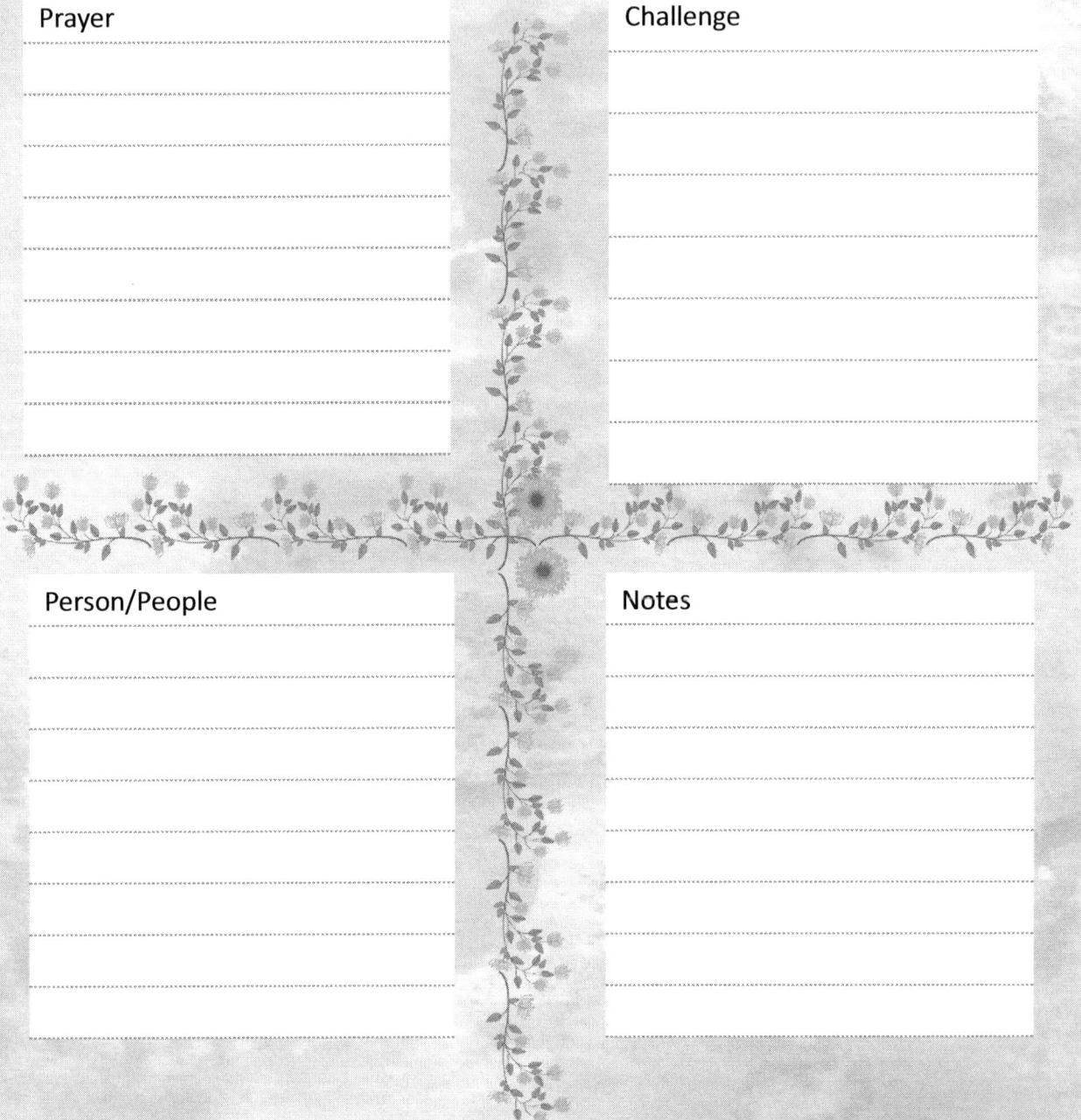

Bible Discussions

Prayer

Challenge

Person/People

Notes

Bible Reading Plan

☐   Text

☐   Text

☐   Text

☐   Text

☐   Text

☐   Text

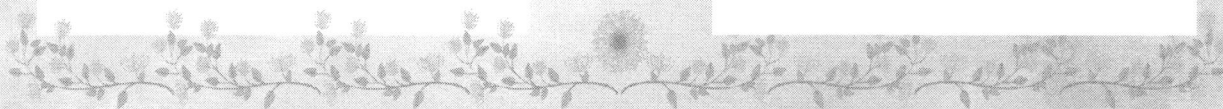

Inspirations

This Week I'm Praying For

Prayer

Enter his gates with thanksgiving
and his courts with praise;
give thanks to him and praise his name.
For the Lord is good and his love endures forever;
his faithfulness continues through all generations.
Psalm 100:4-5

This week I am Thankful For

Things I Learned

My Prayer Calendar

Sun

Mon

Tues

Wed

Thurs

Fri

Sat

Notes

Prayers for our children

My Prayer

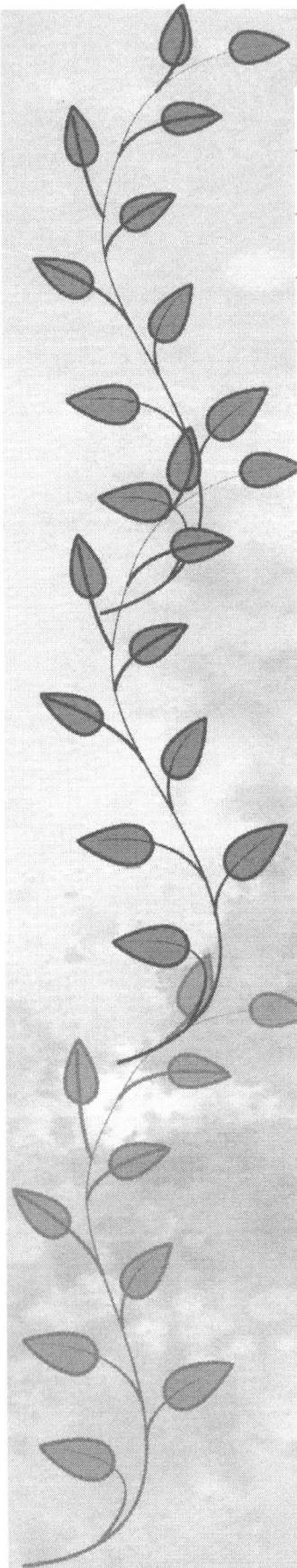

Bible Discussions

Prayer

Challenge

Person/People

Notes

Bible Reading Plan

- [ ] Text
- [ ] Text
- [ ] Text

- [ ] Text
- [ ] Text
- [ ] Text

Inspirations

This Week I'm Praying For

Prayer

I thank and praise you, God of my ancestors:
You have given me wisdom and power,
you have made known to me what we asked of you,
you have made known to us the dream of the king.

Daniel 2:23

This week I am Thankful For

Things I Learned

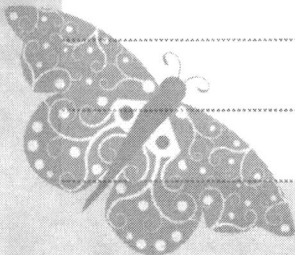

My Prayer Calendar

Sun

Mon

Tues

Wed

Thurs

Fri

Sat

Notes

Prayers for our children

My Prayer

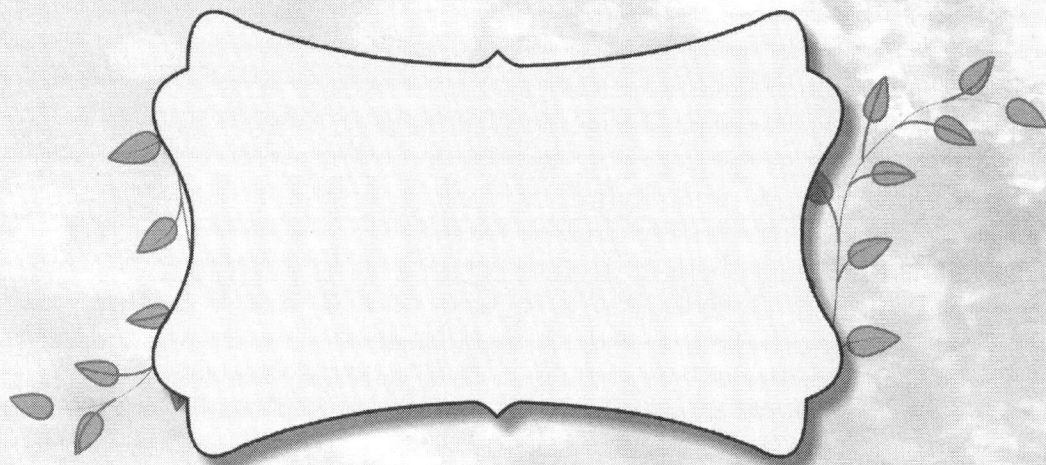

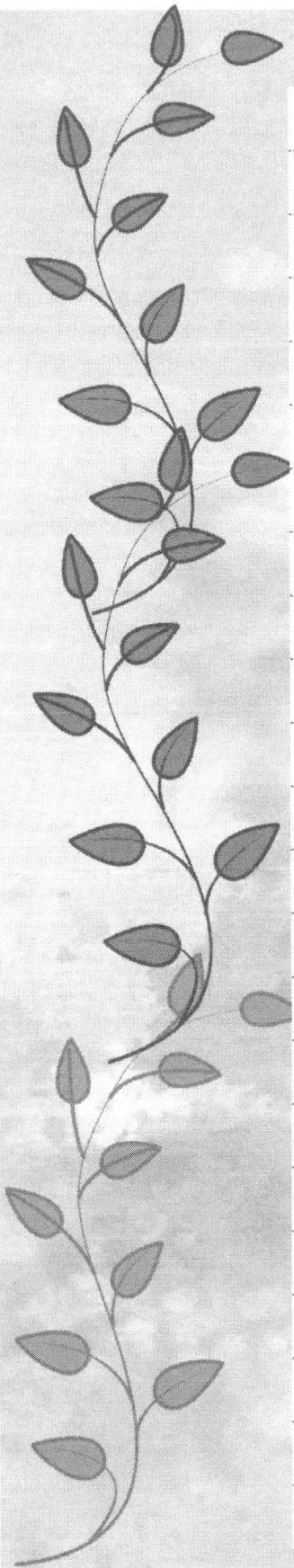

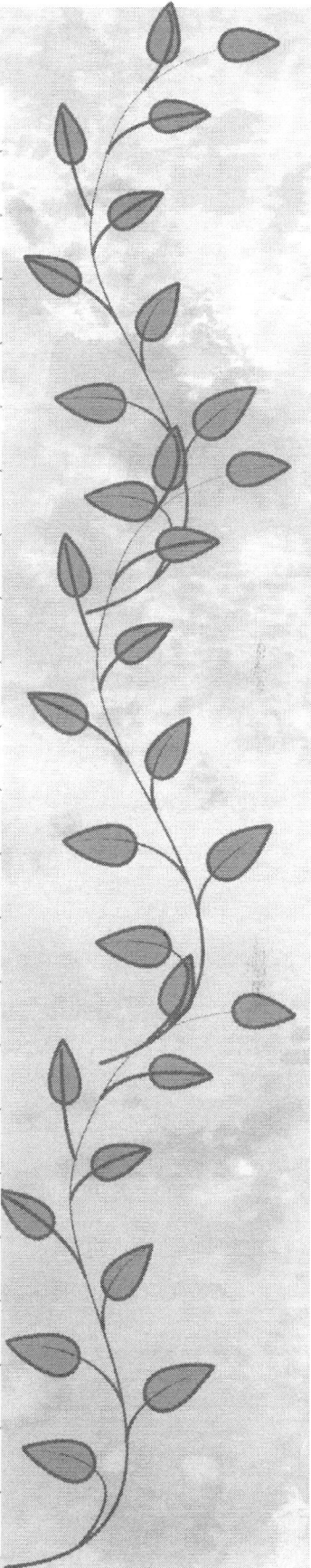

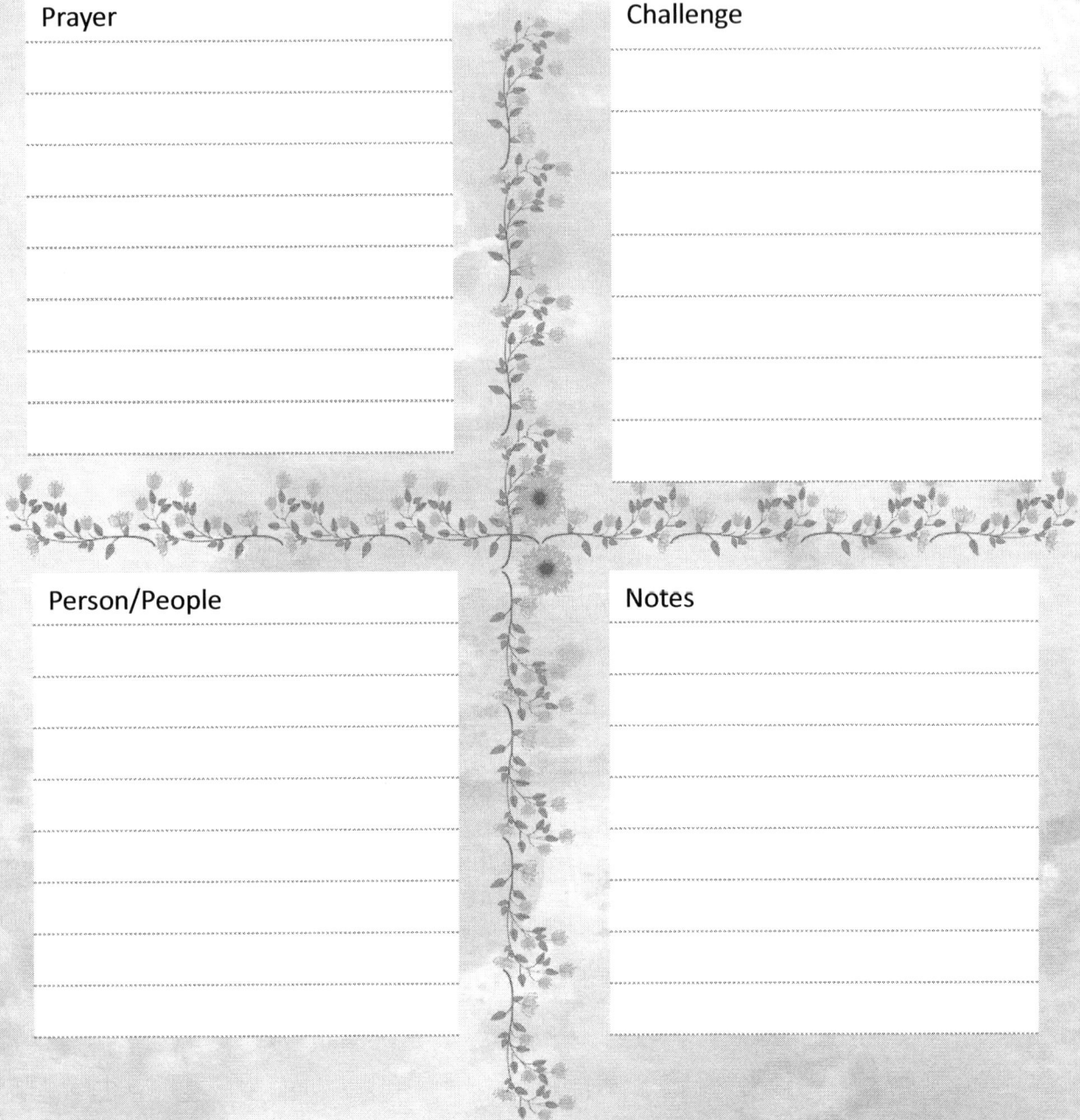

Bible Discussions

Prayer

Challenge

Person/People

Notes

Bible Reading Plan

☐ Text

☐ Text

☐ Text

☐ Text

☐ Text

☐ Text

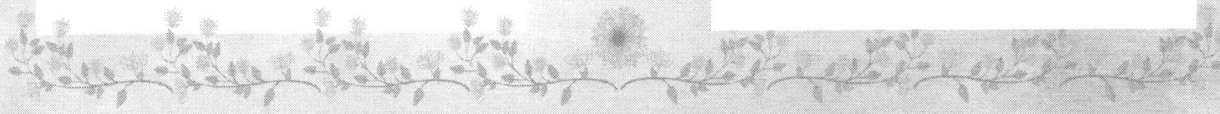

Inspirations

This Week I'm Praying For

Prayer

Let them give thanks to the Lord for his unfailing love
and his wonderful deeds for mankind.
Let them sacrifice thank offerings
and tell of his works with songs of joy.
Psalm 107:21-22

This week I am Thankful For

Things I Learned

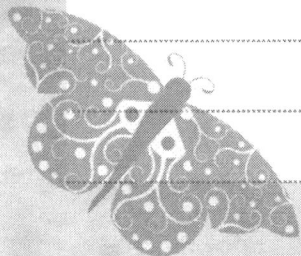

My Prayer Calendar

Sun

Mon

Tues

Wed

Thurs

Fri

Sat

Notes

Prayers for our children

My Prayer

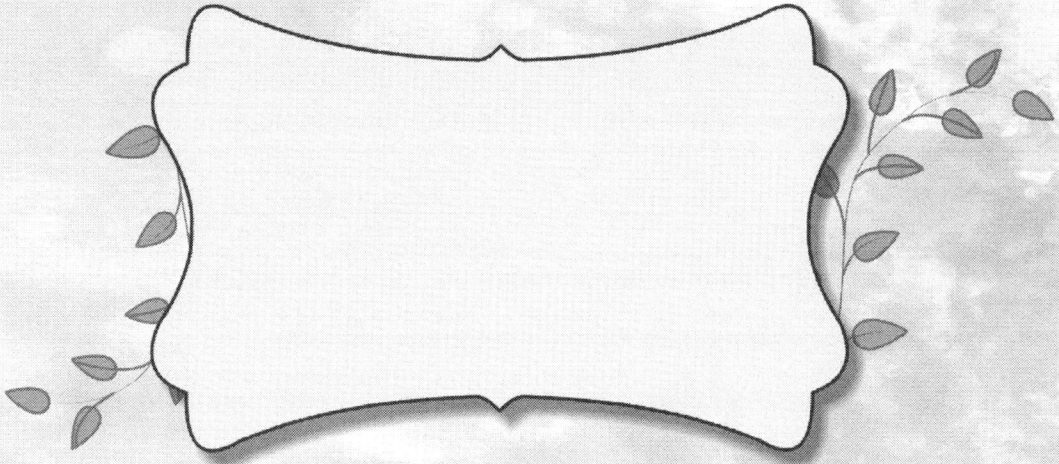

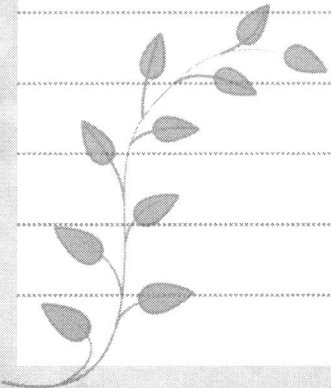

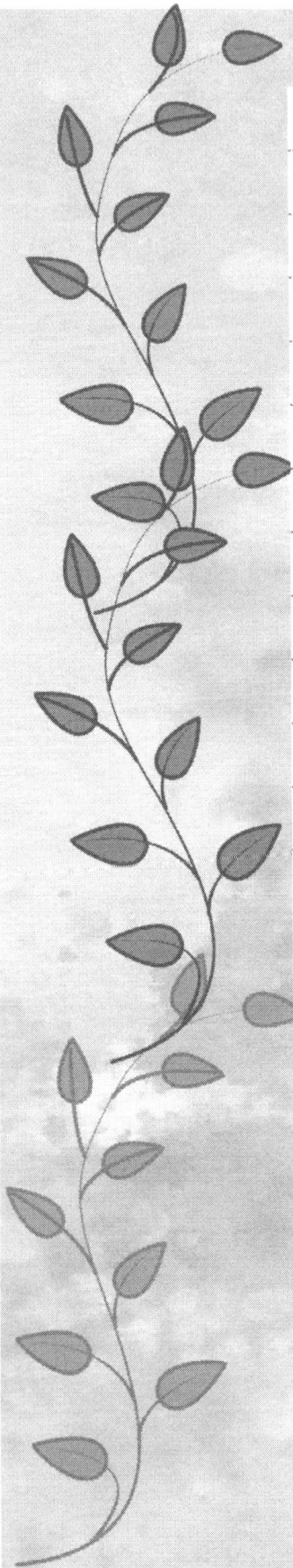

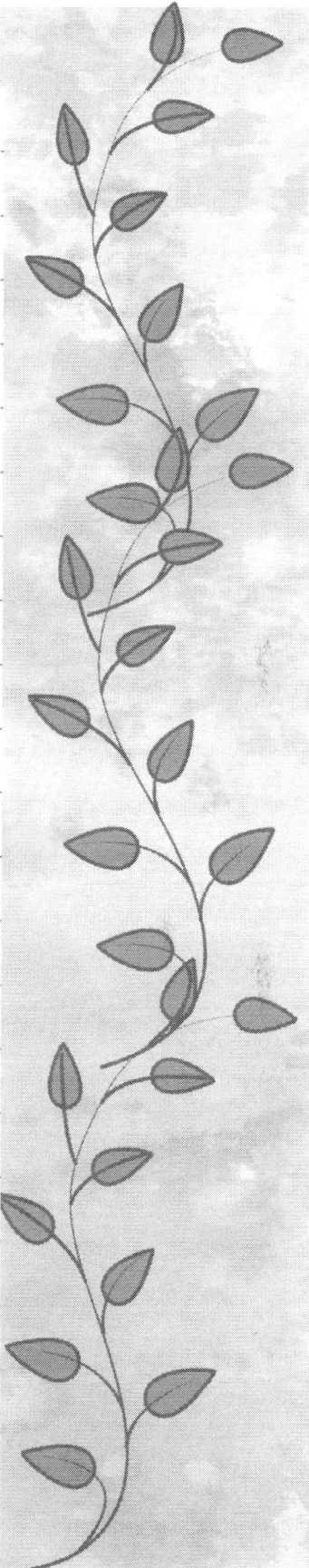

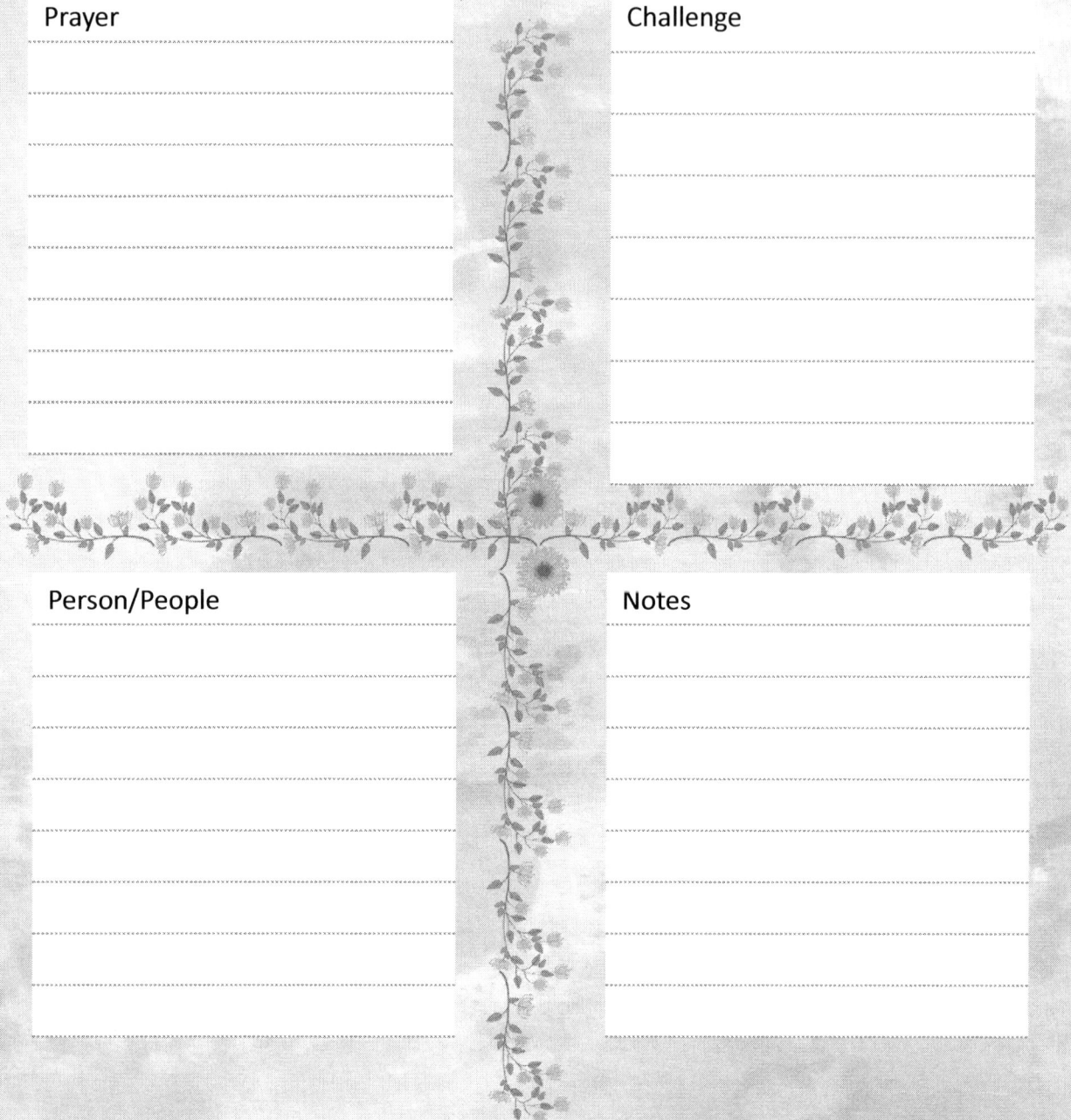

Bible Discussions

Prayer

Challenge

Person/People

Notes

Bible Reading Plan

☐ Text

☐ Text

☐ Text

☐ Text

☐ Text

☐ Text

Inspirations

This Week I'm Praying For

Prayer

Do not get drunk on wine, which leads to debauchery. Instead, be filled with the Spirit, speaking to one another with psalms, hymns, and songs from the Spirit. Sing and make music from your heart to the Lord, always giving thanks to God the Father for everything, in the name of our Lord Jesus Christ.

Ephesians 5:18-20

This week I am Thankful For

Things I Learned

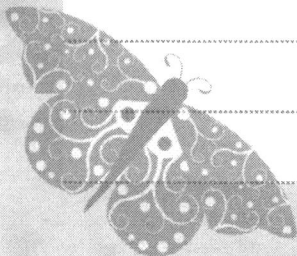

My Prayer Calendar

Sun

Mon

Tues

Wed

Thurs

Fri

Sat

Notes

Prayers for our children

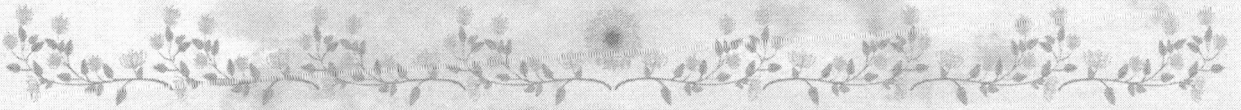

My Prayer

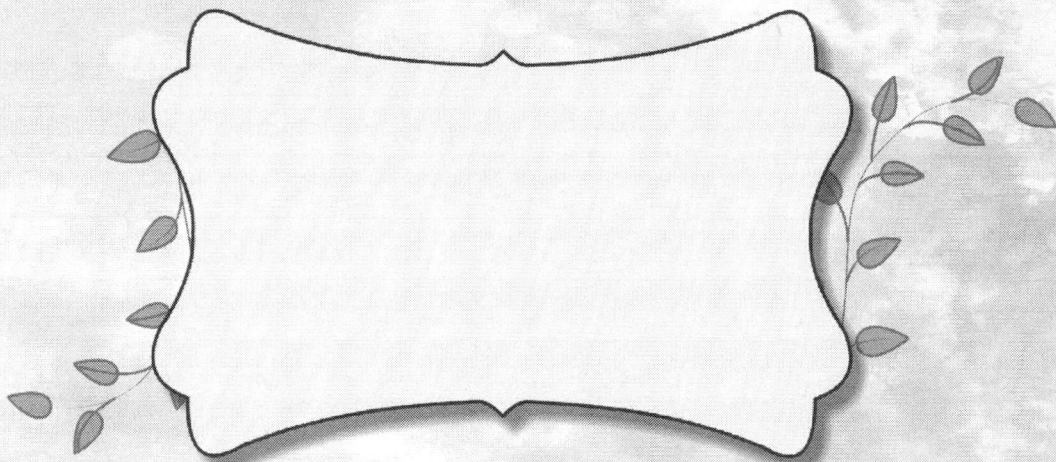

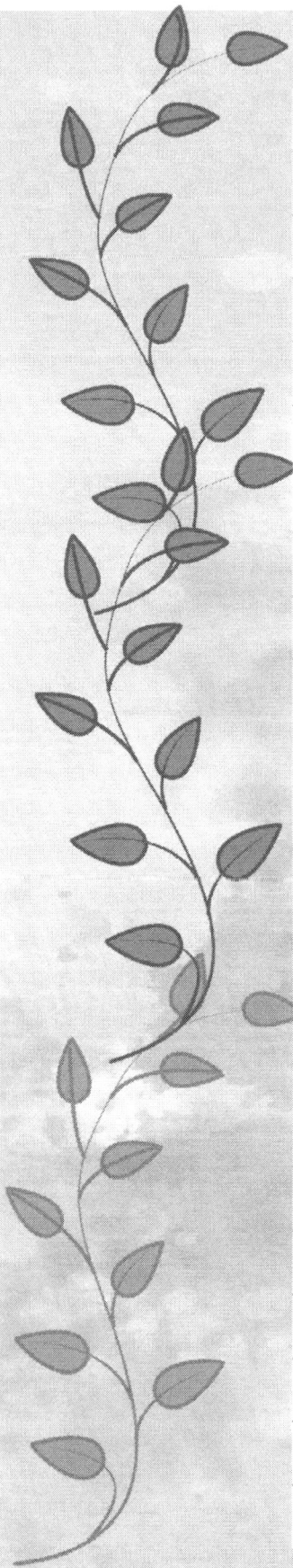

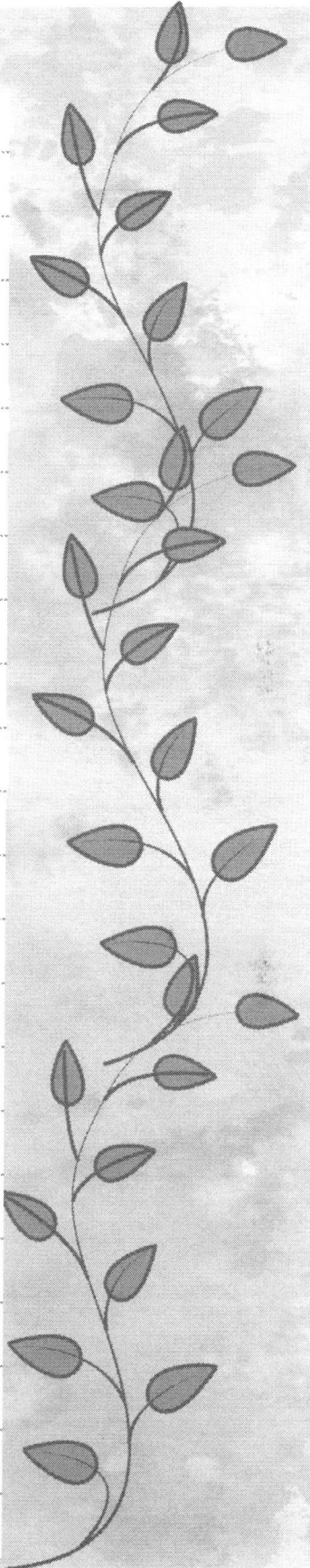

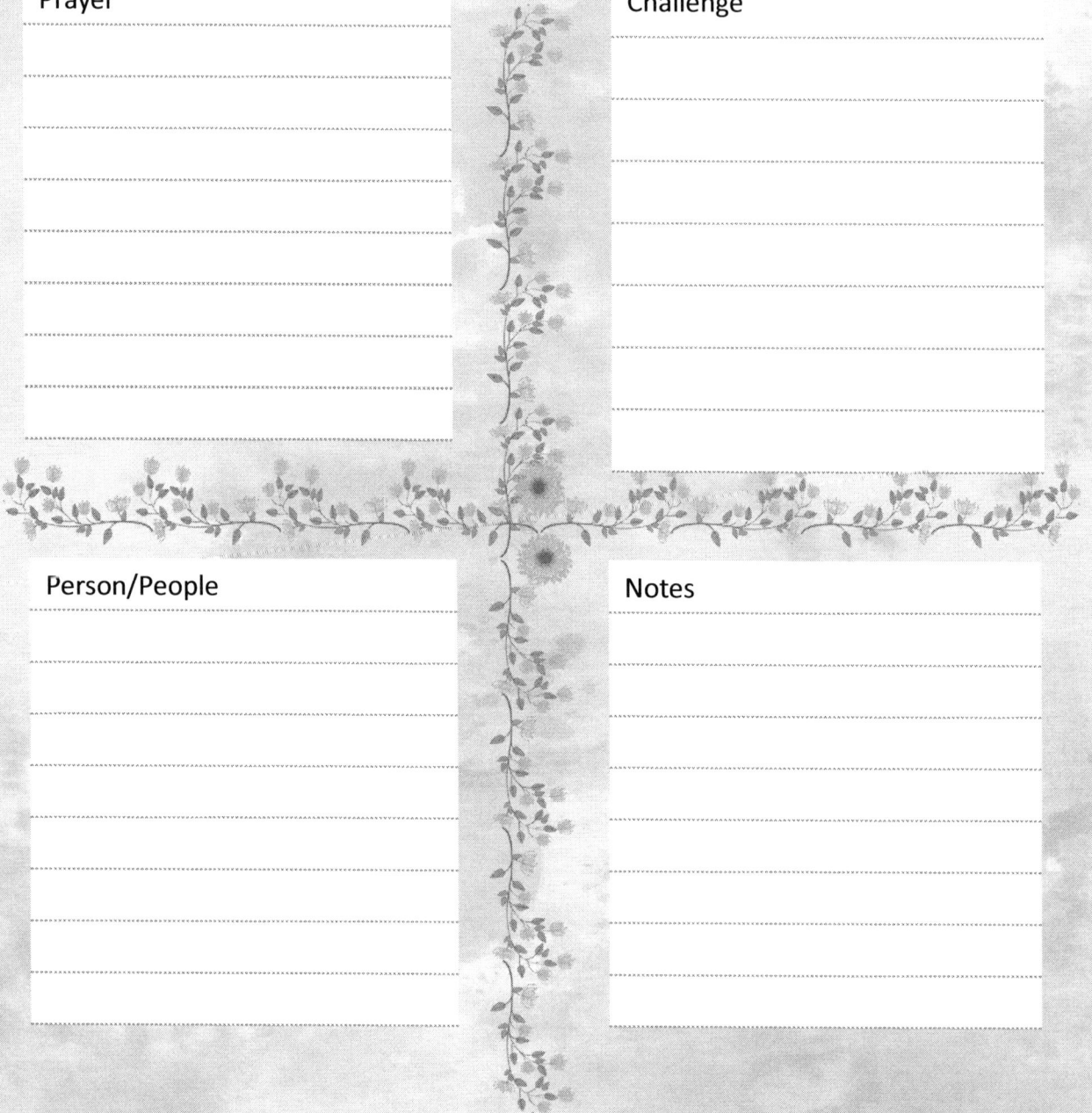

Bible Discussions

Prayer

Challenge

Person/People

Notes

Bible Reading Plan

- ☐ Text
- ☐ Text
- ☐ Text

- ☐ Text
- ☐ Text
- ☐ Text

Inspirations

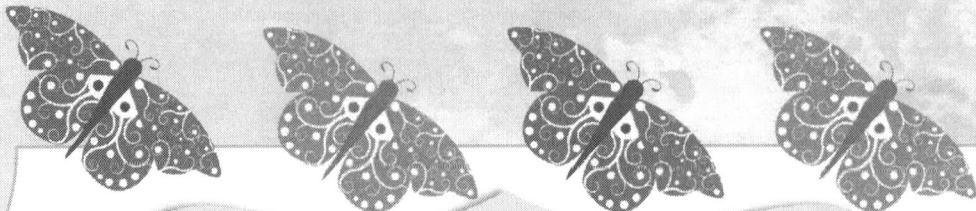

This Week I'm Praying For

Prayer

Through Jesus, therefore, let us continually offer to God a sacrifice of praise — the fruit of lips that openly profess his name. And do not forget to do good and to share with others, for with such sacrifices God is pleased.

Hebrews 13:15-16

This week I am Thankful For

Things I Learned

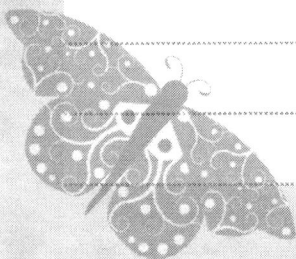

My Prayer Calendar

Sun

Mon

Tues

Wed

Thurs

Fri

Sat

Notes

Prayers for our children

My Prayer

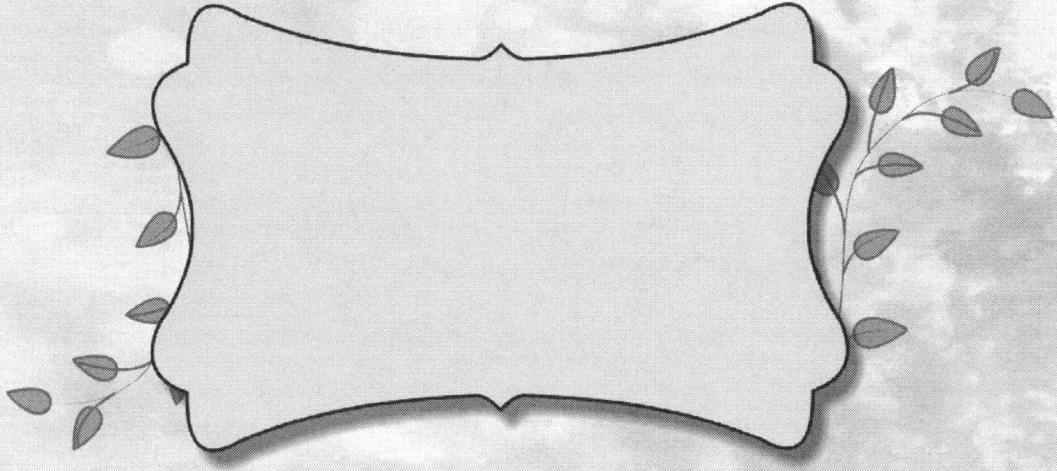

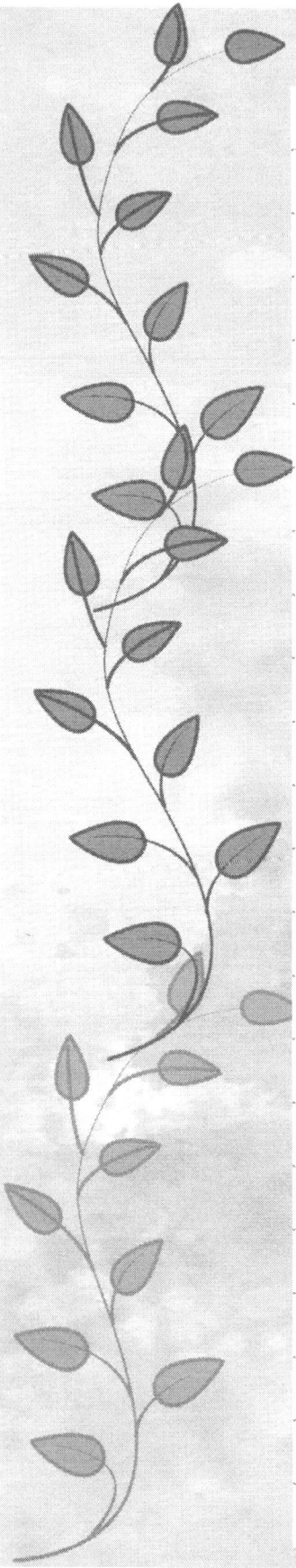

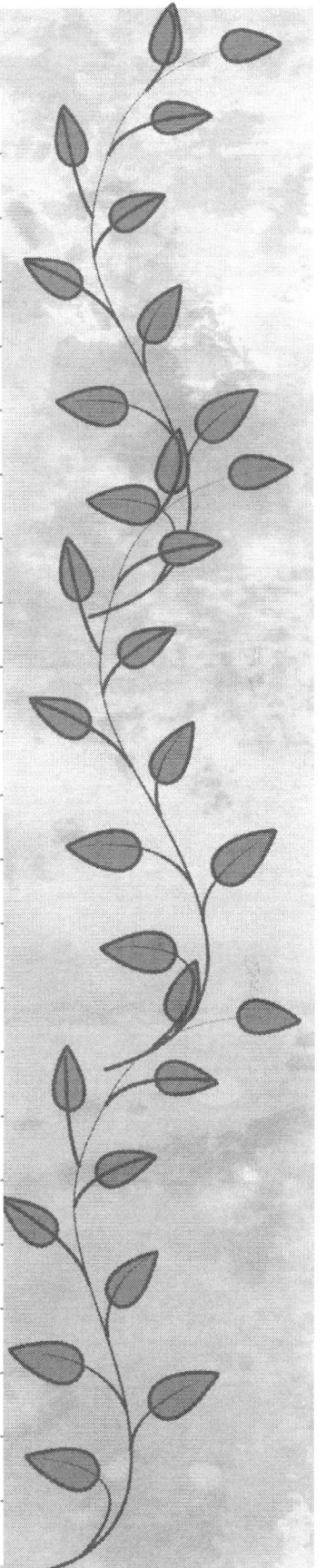

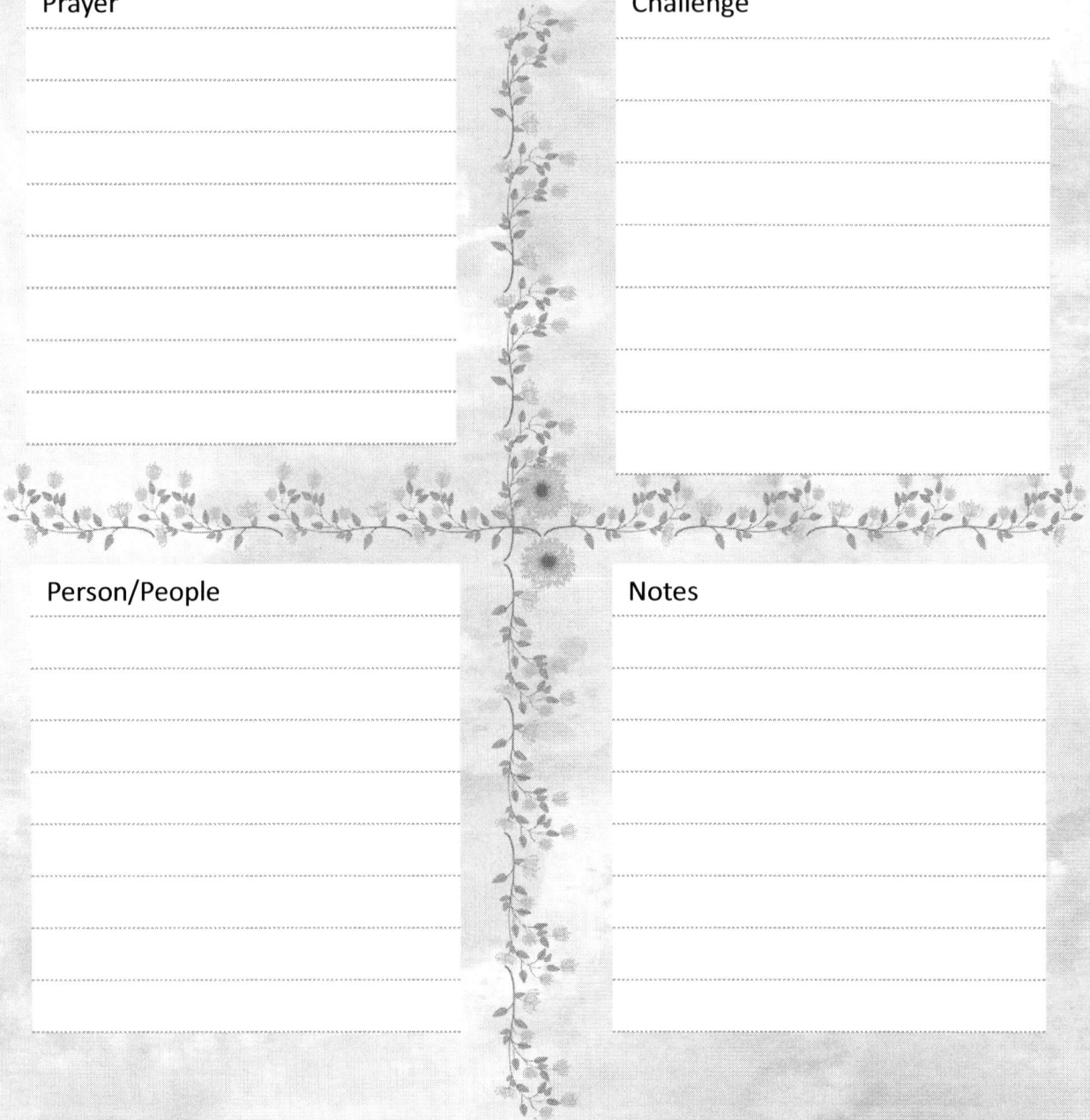

Bible Discussions

Prayer

Challenge

Person/People

Notes

Bible Reading Plan

☐ Text

☐ Text

☐ Text

☐ Text

☐ Text

☐ Text

Inspirations

This Week I'm Praying For

Prayer

When the peace of Christ rules in our hearts, thankfulness overflows. Even in the darkest of times, we can praise God for his love, his sovereignty, and his promise to be near us when we call

Psalm 145:18

This week I am Thankful For

Things I Learned

My Prayer Calendar

Sun

Mon

Tues

Wed

Thurs

Fri

Sat

Notes

Prayers for our children

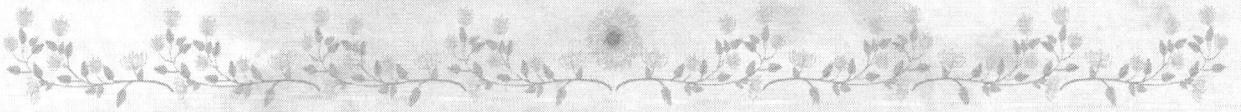

My Prayer

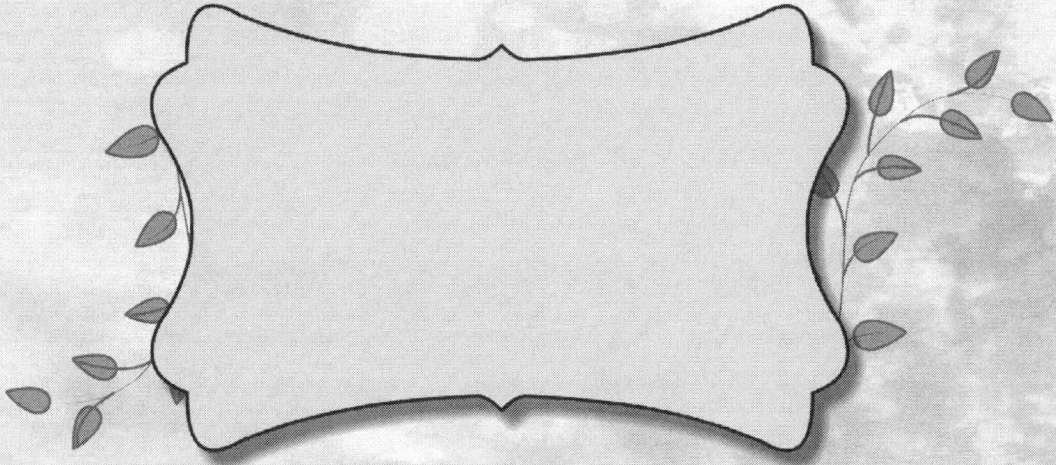

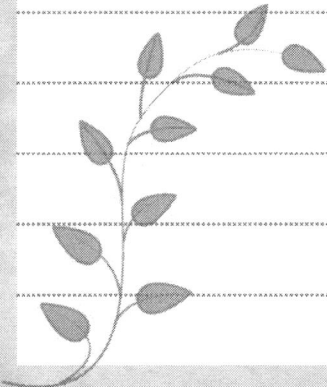

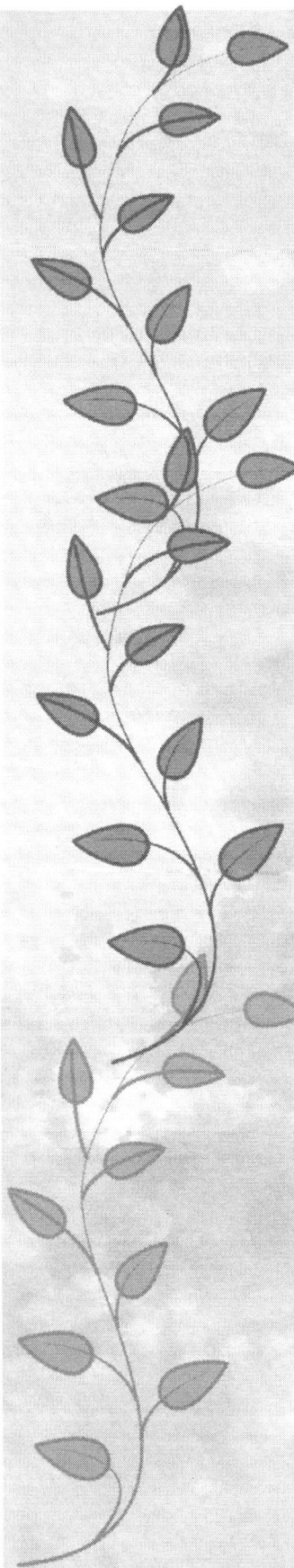

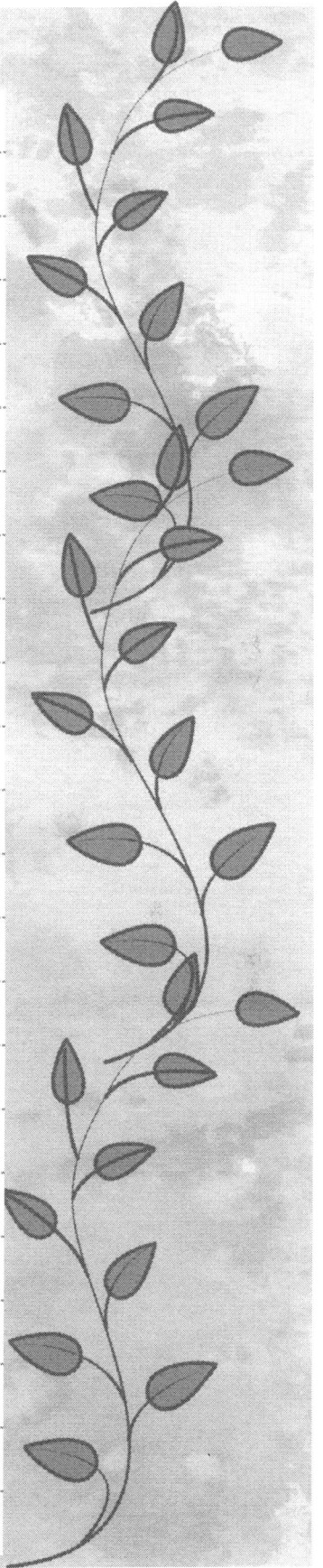

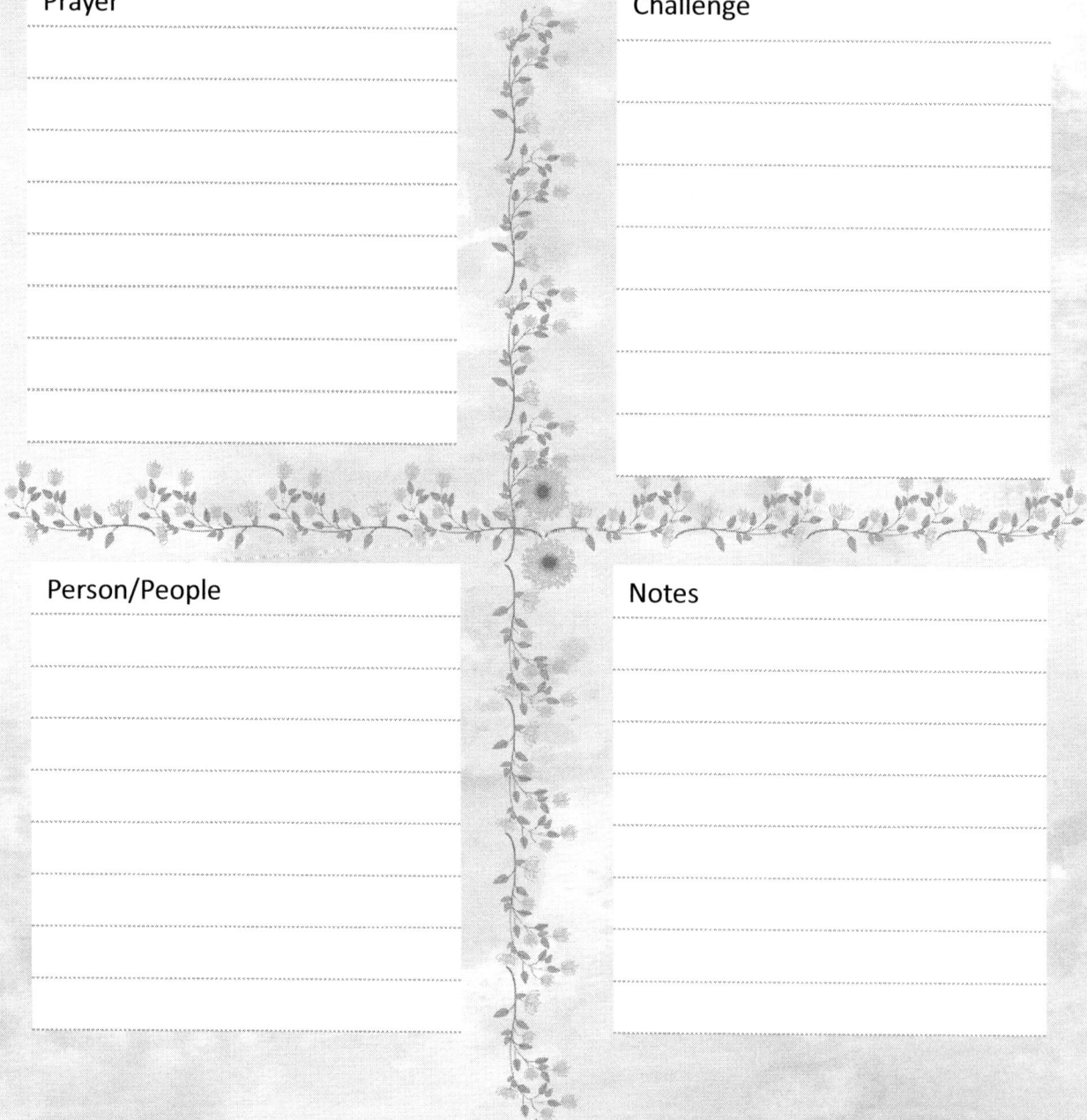

Bible Discussions

Prayer

Challenge

Person/People

Notes

Bible Reading Plan

☐ Text

☐ Text

☐ Text

☐ Text

☐ Text

☐ Text

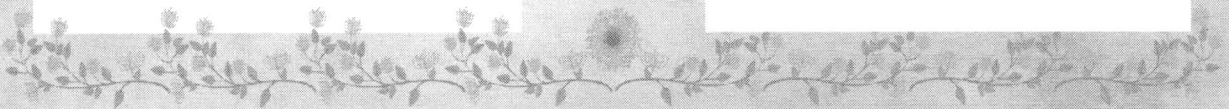

Inspirations

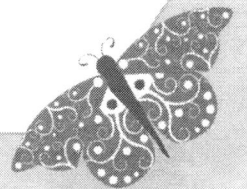

This Week I'm Praying For

Prayer

Let the peace of Christ rule in your hearts, since as members of one body you were called to peace. And be thankful. Let the message of Christ dwell among you richly as you teach and admonish one another with all wisdom through psalms, hymns, and songs from the Spirit, singing to God with gratitude in your hearts. And whatever you do, whether in word or deed, do it all in the name of the Lord Jesus, giving thanks to God the Father through him.

Colossians 3:15-17

This week I am Thankful For

Things I Learned

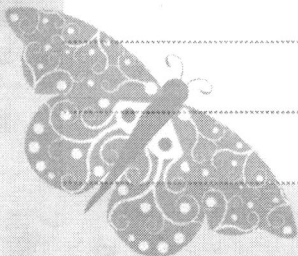

My Prayer Calendar

Sun

Mon

Tues

Wed

Thurs

Fri

Sat

Notes

Prayers for our children

My Prayer

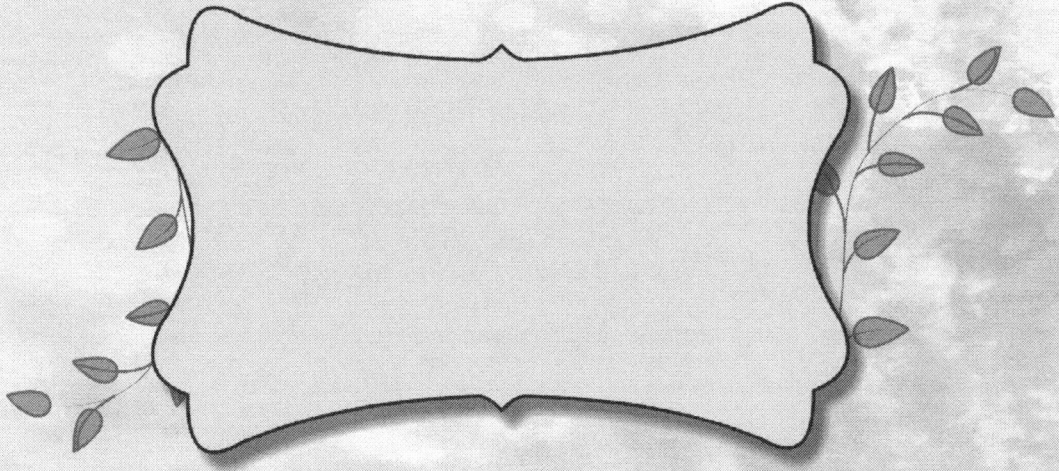

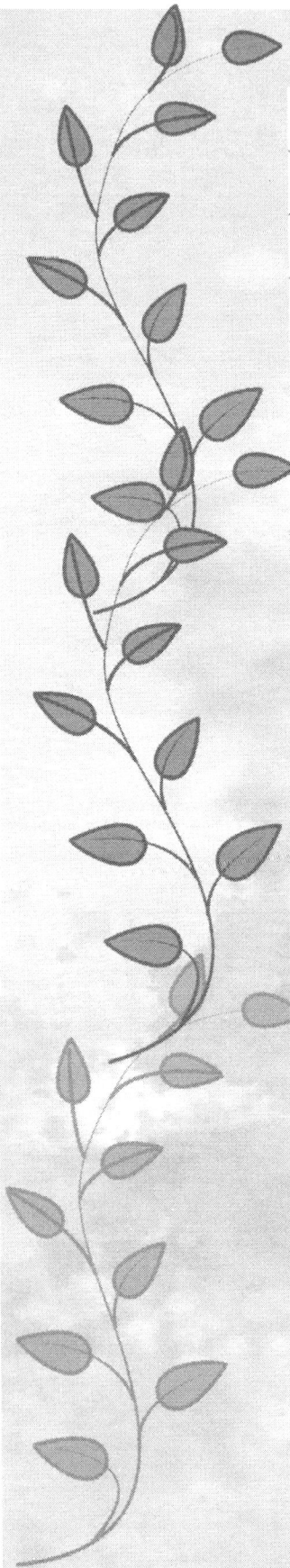

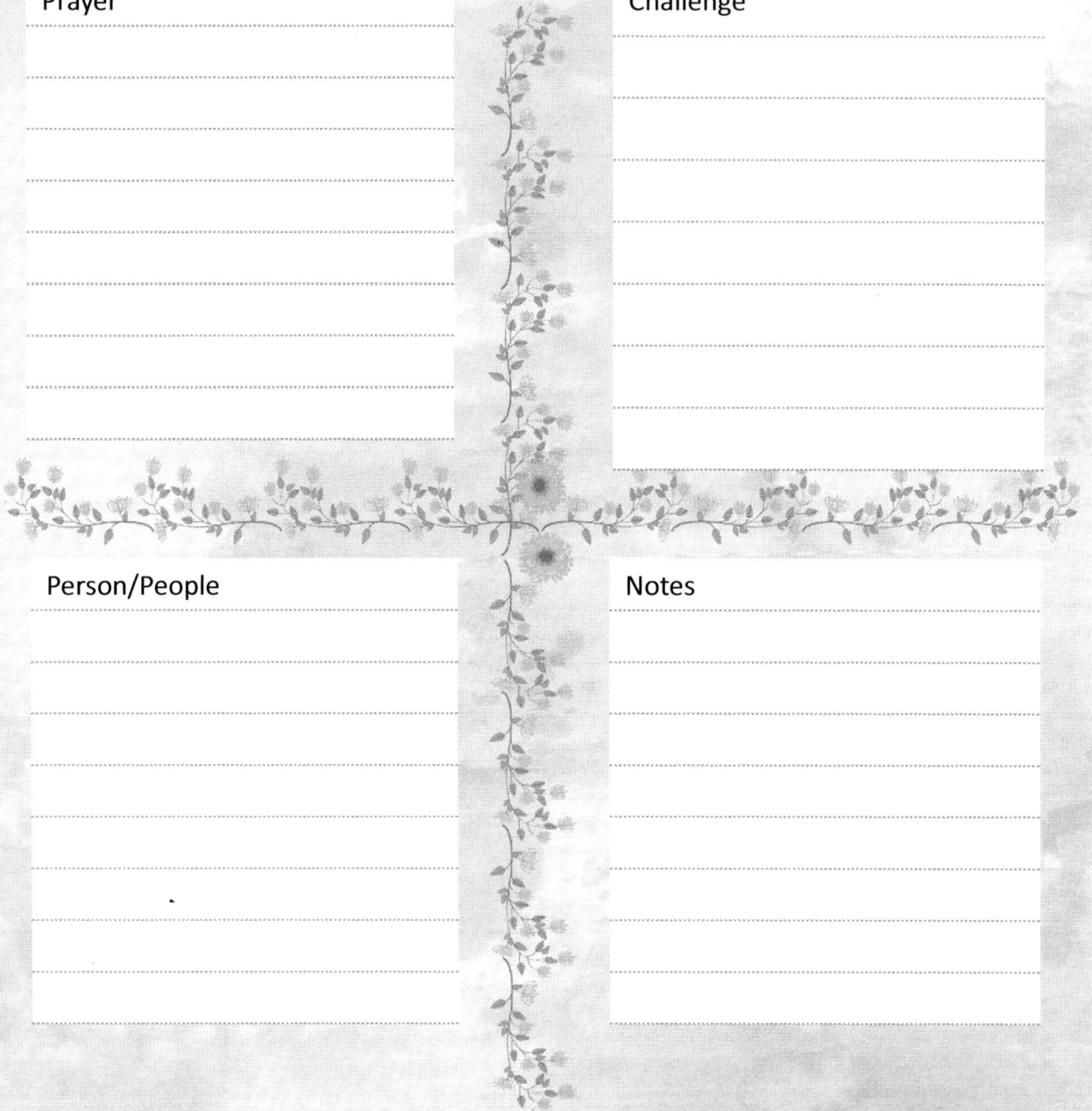

Bible Discussions

Prayer

Challenge

Person/People

Notes

Bible Reading Plan

- ☐ Text
- ☐ Text
- ☐ Text

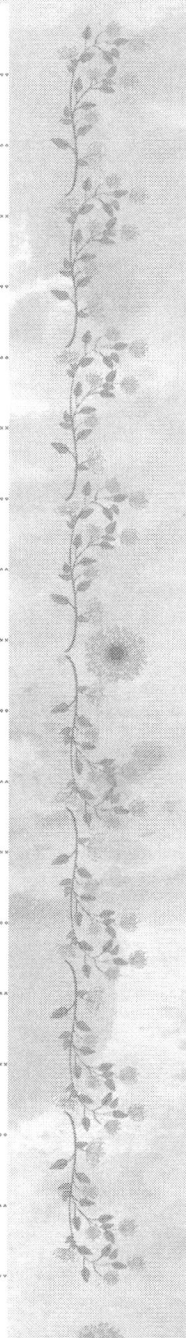

- ☐ Text
- ☐ Text
- ☐ Text

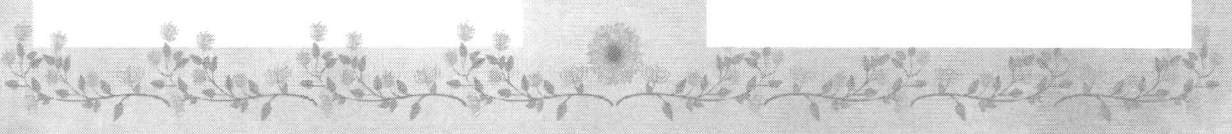

Inspirations

This Week I'm Praying For

Prayer

Do not be anxious about anything, but in every situation, by prayer and petition, with thanksgiving, present your requests to God. And the peace of God, which transcends all understanding, will guard your hearts and your minds in Christ Jesus.

Philippians 4:6-7

This week I am Thankful For

Things I Learned

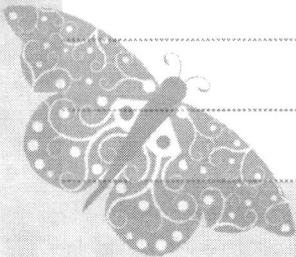

My Prayer Calendar

Sun

Mon

Tues

Wed

Thurs

Fri

Sat

Notes

Prayers for our children

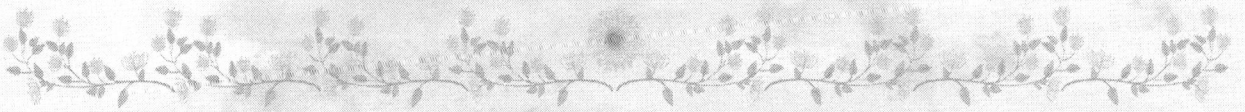

My Prayer

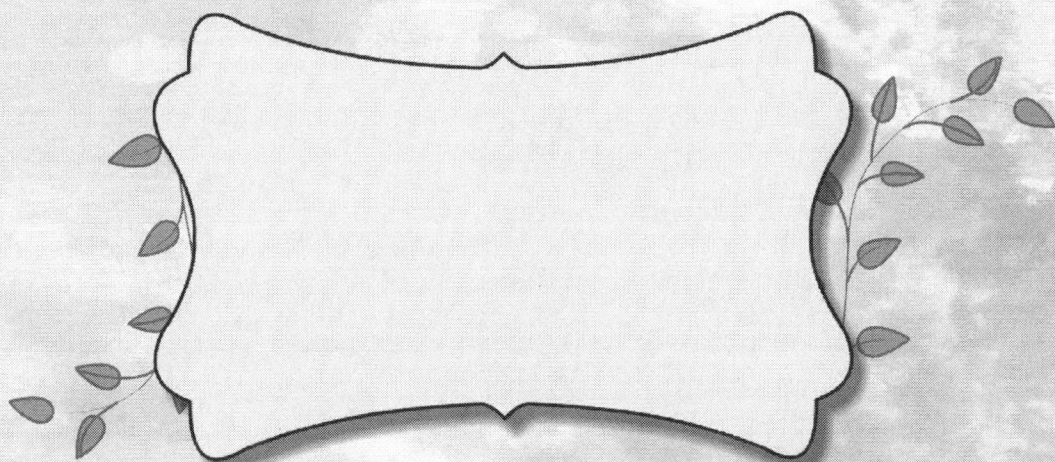

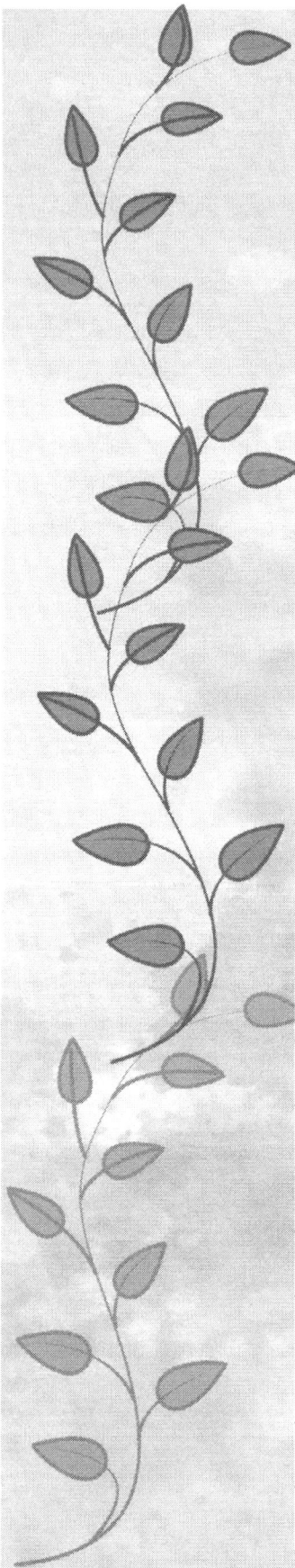

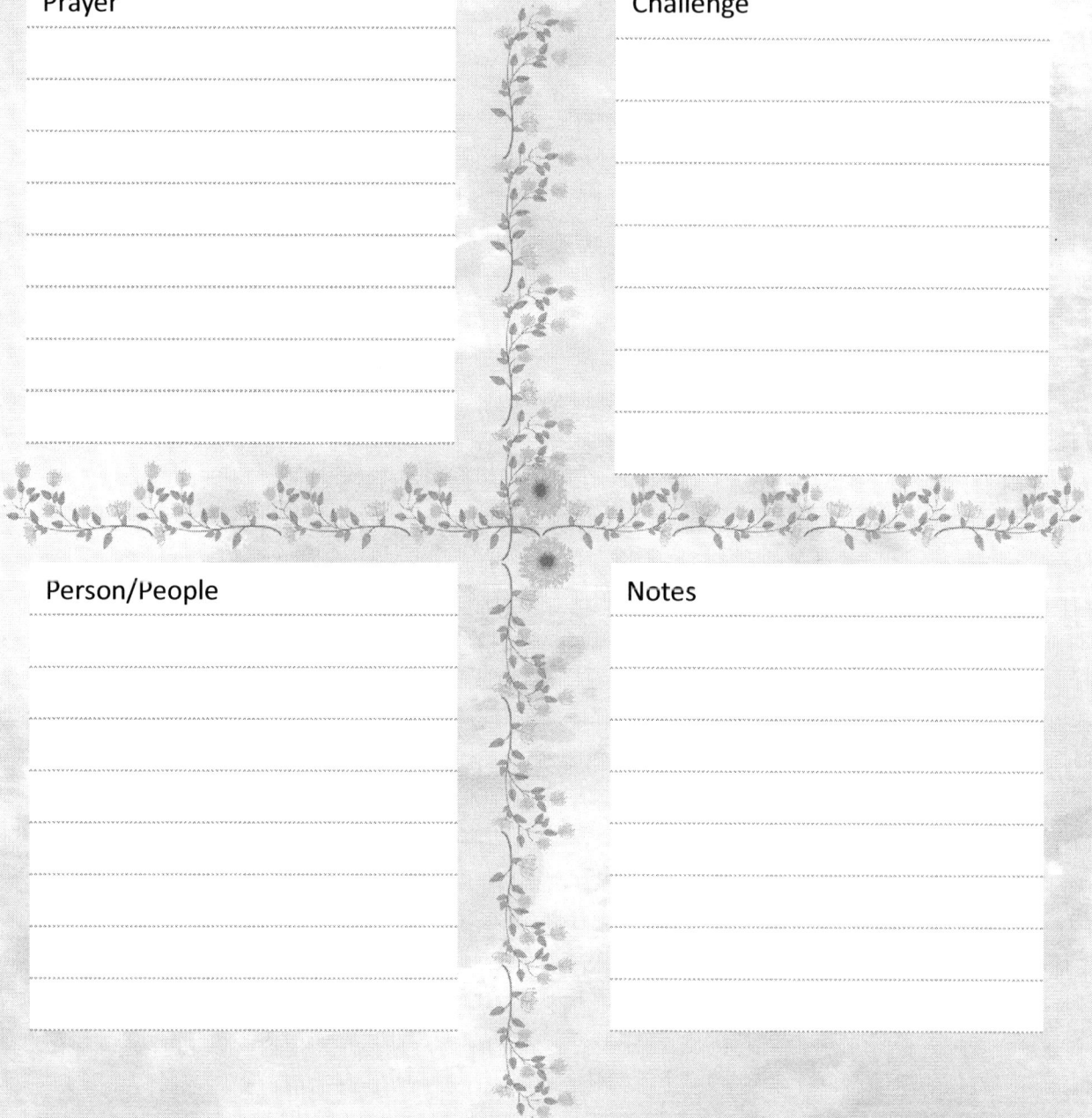

Bible Discussions

Prayer

Challenge

Person/People

Notes

Bible Reading Plan

- ☐ Text
- ☐ Text
- ☐ Text

- ☐ Text
- ☐ Text
- ☐ Text

Inspirations

This Week I'm Praying For

Prayer

Therefore, since we are receiving a kingdom that cannot be shaken, let us be thankful, and so worship God acceptably with reverence and awe, for our "God is a consuming fire."

Hebrews 12:28-29

This week I am Thankful For

Things I Learned

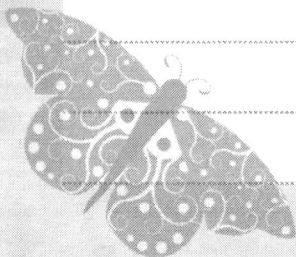

My Prayer Calendar

Sun

Mon

Tues

Wed

Thurs

Fri

Sat

Notes

Prayers for our children

My Prayer

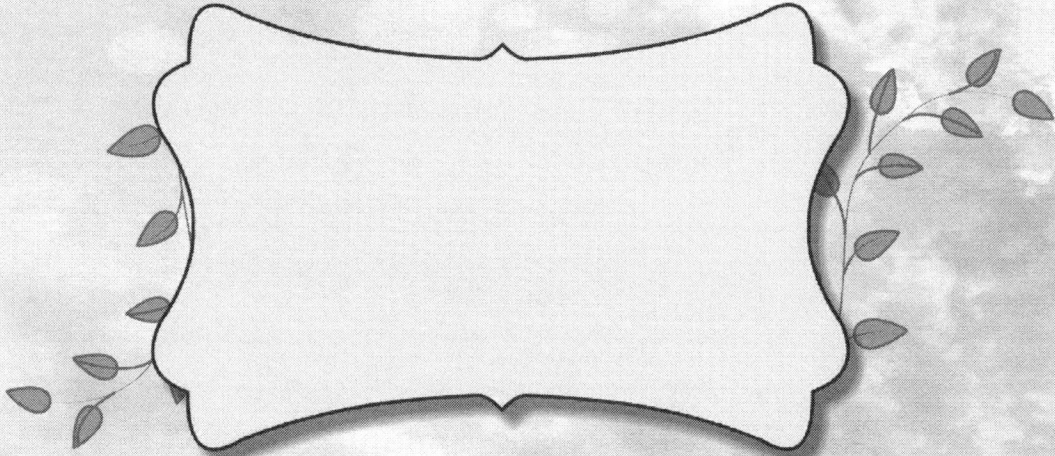

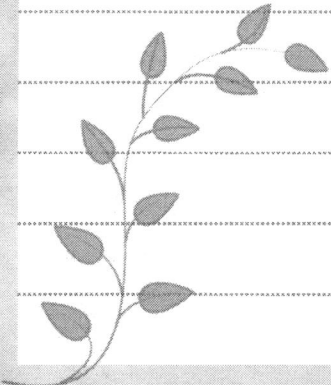

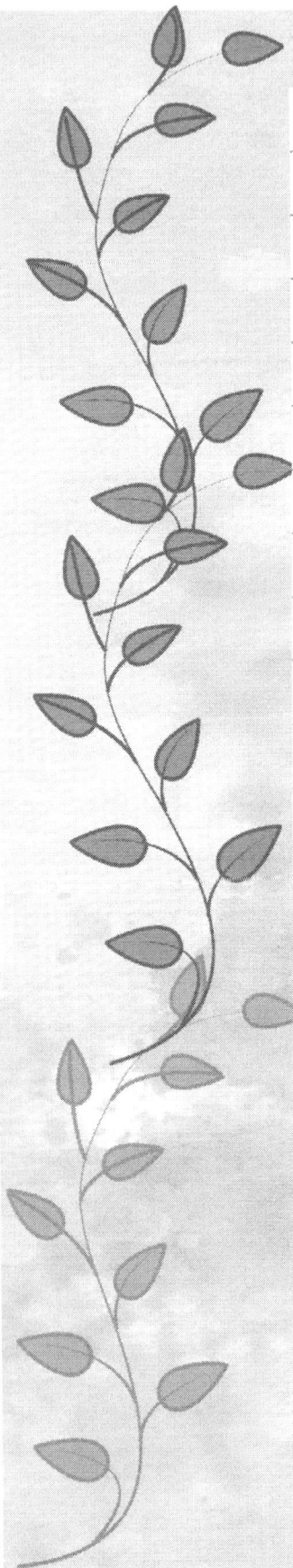

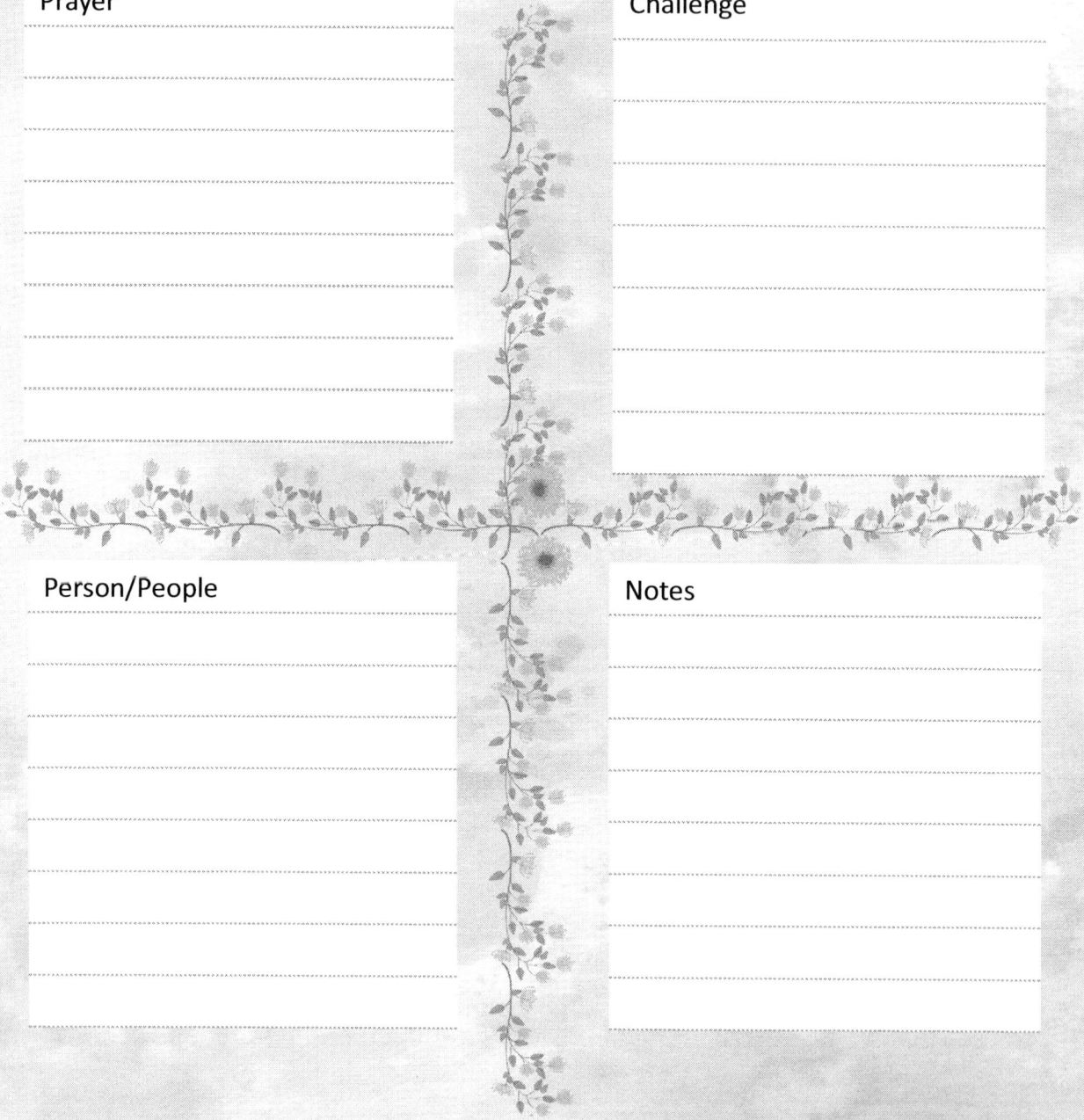

Bible Discussions

Prayer

Challenge

Person/People

Notes

Bible Reading Plan

☐ Text

☐ Text

☐ Text

☐ Text

☐ Text

☐ Text

Inspirations

This Week I'm Praying For

Prayer

So then, just as you received Christ Jesus as Lord, continue to live your lives in him, rooted and built up in him, strengthened in the faith as you were taught, and overflowing with thankfulness..

Colossians 2:6-7

This week I am Thankful For

Things I Learned

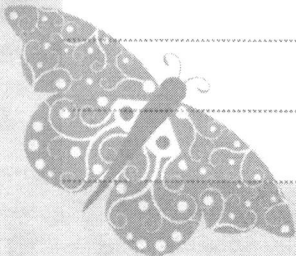

My Prayer Calendar

Sun

Mon

Tues

Wed

Thurs

Fri

Sat

Notes

Prayers for our children

My Prayer

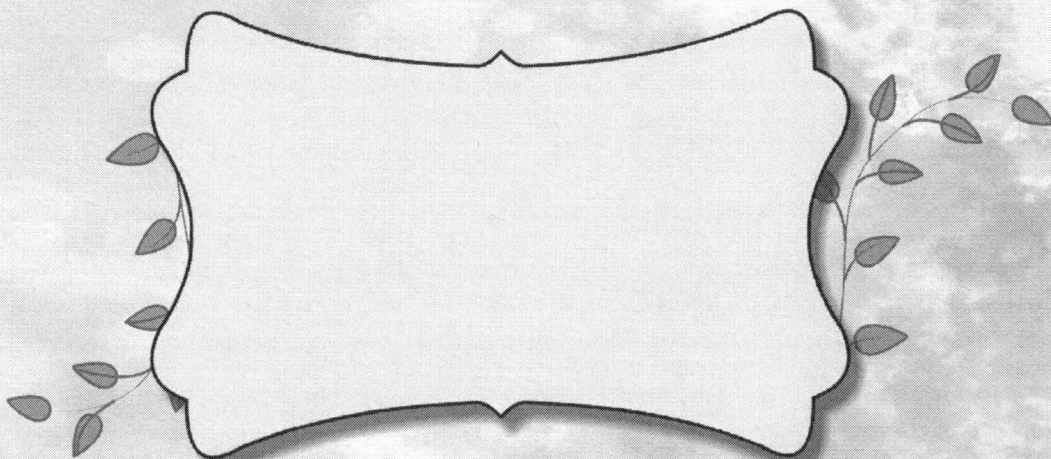

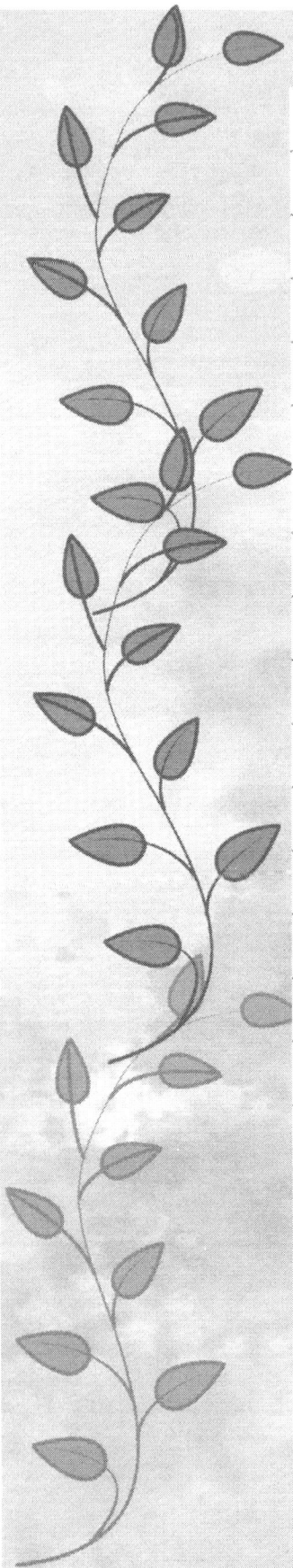

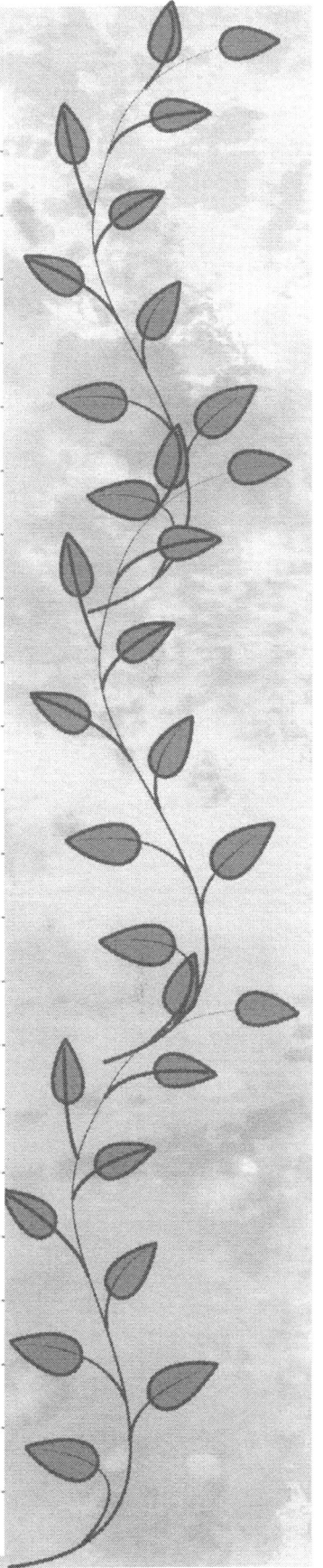

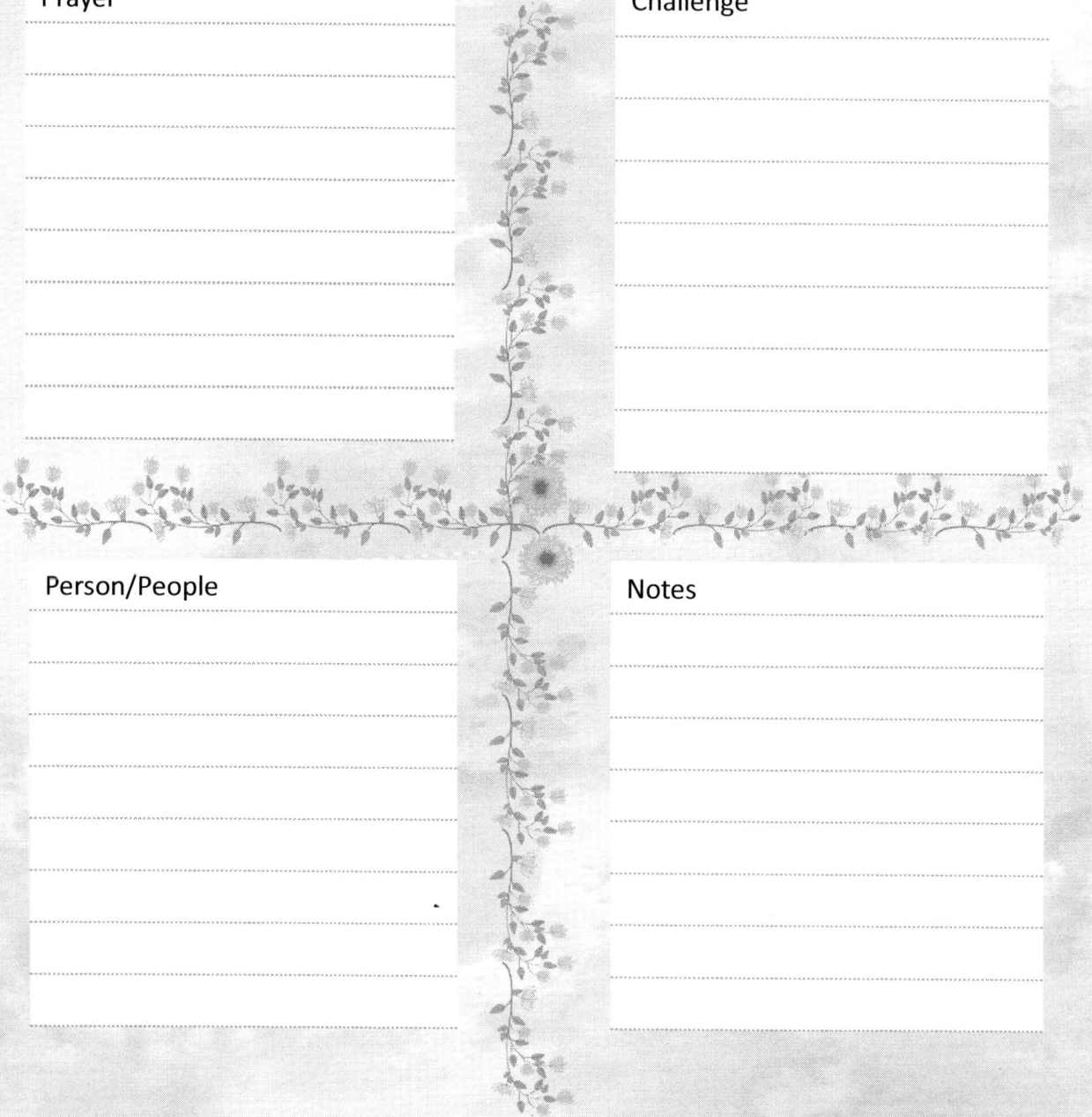

Bible Discussions

Prayer

Challenge

Person/People

Notes

Bible Reading Plan

☐ Text

☐ Text

☐ Text

☐ Text

☐ Text

☐ Text

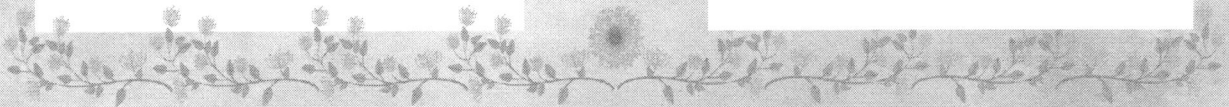

Inspirations

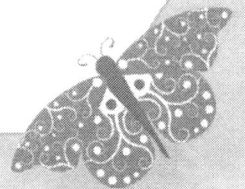

Thank you, Lord, for your peace that transcends understanding and your love that endures forever. Amen!

Made in the USA
Las Vegas, NV
09 July 2022